SKY LIFE
Living in Space

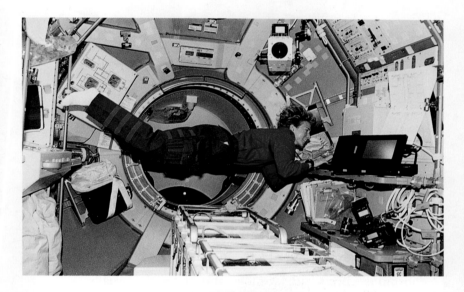

by Miranda Spekes
illustrated by Jeff Lindberg

Harcourt

Orlando Boston Dallas Chicago San Diego

Visit *The Learning Site!*

www.harcourtschool.com

Living in "The Future"

For decades science fiction writers have been imagining what life in space might be like. Images of space stations as enormous wheels with windows and of people casually zooming around in zero gravity are familiar to anyone who has seen movies or watched television shows about the future.

Usually such stories take place many years into the future, at a time when humanity has populated space and when a trip to the moon is as common as an airplane ride across the country. Those stories might not be as far off as you think, however. Astronauts are living in space

today, and with the successful launch of the *International Space Station*, we are learning exactly what it takes for people to live and thrive in space. The future, it seems, is now.

What we will discover aboard the *International Space Station* may someday make it possible for many civilians—not just astronauts—to journey into space and get a taste of the sky life.

Before you sign up for a ticket to the stars, however, you should know that life in space is no picnic. Sure, life in orbit can be a lot of fun, but it is also very challenging, stressful, and in some ways quite hazardous. In fact, getting into space is only half the battle; the other half is surviving your stay.

Mental Fitness

One important requirement for a prospective astronaut has to do with his or her personality. Although astronauts have to be smart and well educated, they also have to be mentally fit for the job. The ability to handle stress may be even more important than astronauts' scientific knowledge. Do they have short tempers? Are they able to get along with others? Do they sometimes get depressed? Are they loners or team players?

Imagine sharing a bedroom with someone you don't know very well. You and that person might start to annoy each other after a few days. Now imagine sharing that same room with *five* people, for months at a time, knowing that none of you can leave. Not only would you share a bedroom, but you would also have to share all of the facilities—the kitchen, the bathroom, the shower, the gym. Privacy would be almost nonexistent, and tempers could flare over the tiniest things. You would have no television, no video games, and not a lot of room for playing sports. Even in the best of circumstances, this arrangement would get on your nerves.

Although the *International Space Station* will eventually be about as big as a football field—131 feet high, 290 feet wide, and 356 feet long—inside there will only be about as much room as you'd find in a 747 jumbo jet. Most of that will be taken up by scientific equipment, life-support systems, and laboratories.

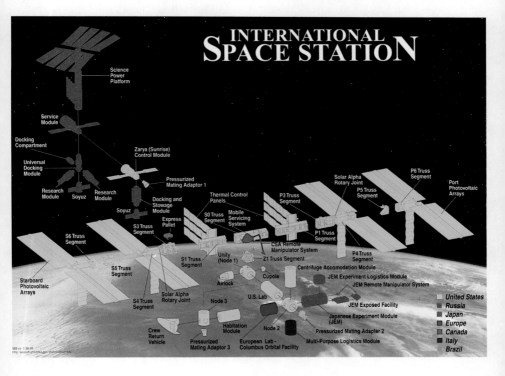

INTERNATIONAL SPACE STATION

Science Power Platform

Service Module

Docking Compartment

Universal Docking Module

Zarya (Sunrise) Control Module

Research Module   Soyuz   Research Module

Soyuz

Pressurized Mating Adaptor 1

Docking and Stowage Module

Express Pallet

S6 Truss Segment

S3 Truss Segment

S5 Truss Segment

Starboard Photovoltaic Arrays

S4 Truss Segment

Solar Alpha Rotary Joint

Solar Alpha Rotary Joint

Thermal Control Panels

S0 Truss Segment

Mobile Servicing System

S1 Truss Segment

Unity (Node 1)

Z1 Truss Segment

Cupola

Airlock

Node 3

Crew Return Vehicle

Pressurized Mating Adaptor 3

Habitation Module

European Lab - Columbus Orbital Facility

U.S. Lab

Node 2

CSA Remote Manipulator System

Centrifuge Accomodation Module

P3 Truss Segment

P5 Truss Segment

P6 Truss Segment

Port Photovoltaic Arrays

P1 Truss Segment

P4 Truss Segment

JEM Experiment Logistics Module

JEM Remote Manipulator System

JEM Exposed Facility

Japanese Experiment Module (JEM)

Pressurized Mating Adapter 2

Multi-Purpose Logistics Module

- United States
- Russia
- Japan
- Europe
- Canada
- Italy
- Brazil

One out of the eight primary modules has been set aside for living space. (The other seven are devoted to research and station operations.) It is hard to maneuver in zero gravity because you can't tell which way is up or down. Navigation's harder still when you are only one of five people floating around in the same tiny area. The simplest activities take more effort than they require on Earth, and you will certainly bump heads with your roommates sometimes.

No number of space station simulations can prepare an astronaut for the isolation of orbital life. Long stays in cramped quarters strain a person psychologically, and that affects relationships among members of the crew.

5

In order to figure out what makes an astronaut mentally fit, psychologists are studying how the Russian astronauts, called cosmonauts, deal with their long stays in space. During one 1982 mission, cosmonaut Valentin Lebedev suffered from insomnia, depression, and anxiety. All of these problems affected Lebedev's relationships with the people he had to deal with: his crewmates and the ground controllers. On another mission in 1994 and 1995, one cosmonaut got so angry over a small disagreement that he stopped talking to his crewmates entirely! Obviously, behavior such as that can cause trouble during a mission. If an astronaut can't work with the people around him or her, nothing can get done.

Salyuts 1-6

The former Soviet Union launched the first space station. The first Salyut space station was put into orbit in April 1971 and fell back to Earth six months later. The station was only about thirty-five feet long and twelve feet wide at its thickest point. Six other Salyuts followed during the 1970s and 1980s. These stations allowed cosmonauts to spend extended periods of time in space and to perform hundreds of experiments.

What sort of psychological makeup does a person need in order to live on a space station? Psychologists suggest that ideal astronauts have the following qualities:

- They are good communicators. They can discuss problems with their crewmates before tensions get too high.
- They are good at working in groups. They need to be able to take on their assigned roles within a team.
- They are aware of the feelings of those around them and will be careful not to offend people of different backgrounds.

Physical Fitness

Astronauts are required to be in top physical condition before they journey into space. The rocket ride from Earth's surface up to a space station is a difficult one. Even if an astronaut is in the best shape of his or her life, it can be very hard for that person to stay fit and healthy in space.

One of the biggest dangers astronauts face while living on a space station is one they cannot even see, something called *bone loss.* Most people think of bones as being hard and unchangeable, but, in fact, bones are living tissue that changes as you grow older or when you exercise. For example, if you lift heavy weights, not only do your muscles grow bigger, but your bones grow stronger, too.

When an astronaut spends a long period of time in space, the opposite happens: his or her bones grow weaker. Because gravity is no longer pulling on an astronaut's body, the body no longer has any weight to carry around. The body begins to break down bone tissue and the bones become fragile, often breaking easily.

This change in bone density is similar to what happens when people contract a bone disease called osteoporosis. If bones do not receive enough calcium and other minerals, they, too, will become fragile.

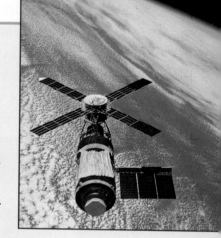

Skylab

The United States launched *Skylab* in May 1973. Nearly eighty-five feet long and twenty-two feet wide, it provided astronauts with a place to learn about zero gravity and its effects on people. *Skylab* also allowed astronauts to view the sun and other stars in ways that are impossible from Earth's surface and to prove that people could live and work in space for long periods of time.

Over the next six years, astronauts spent more than 170 days on the station and completed more than 300 experiments. *Skylab* fell back to Earth in July 1979.

To counteract bone loss, astronauts must spend a large part of each day exercising on stationary bikes and tread-mills. On the space station *Mir* the cosmonauts were required to exercise for two-and-a-half hours each day. While these aerobic workouts help combat bone loss some-what, they are not enough. Scientists are trying to find other ways to fight this problem. The key seems to lie in making the muscles do more work, as you do when you lift heavy weights. However, in zero gravity, where everything is weightless, "weight lifting" is meaningless. So what can astronauts do to keep themselves healthy and strong?

The Russians tried one solution. On *Mir* cosmonauts wore specially designed jumpsuits with strong rubber bands woven into them so that every body movement required muscle exertion. It is not yet clear how much these suits halted bone loss, however.

Mir

The Russians began building *Mir* in 1986. *Mir* was an inspiration both for the design and construction of the *International Space Station* and for the example it provided of international cooperation. Close to a hundred astronauts visited *Mir*, some of them Americans. Many cosmonauts stayed in the station for periods longer than six months, carrying out experiments that lasted weeks, months, or even years. The Russians brought *Mir* back to Earth in March, 2001.

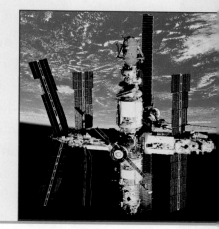

Another solution for bone loss might come from science fiction novels and movies. Why not *rotate* space stations? If a space station is spun quickly enough (like a giant wheel), the rotation creates *centrifugal force*. Centrifugal force pushes everything away from the center. (If you hold a bucket of water by the handle and swing it very quickly in a circle, centrifugal force holds the water against the bottom of the bucket.) On a big space station, centrifugal force could create the illusion of gravity, so that the outside wall becomes "down" and the center of the station becomes "up." This "artificial gravity" would force the astronauts to carry their body weight, just as they do on Earth.

Whether one of these options becomes a standard in space station construction or whether science comes up with some other high-tech solution, bone loss is a serious hazard of life in space that makes long-term habitation of space an impossibility—for now.

Cosmic Radiation and Solar Radiation

If you have ever had a sunburn, you know that the sun's rays are harmful. For the most part, Earth's atmosphere blocks out the worst of the sun's ultraviolet rays, as well as harmful cosmic radiation such as gamma rays and X rays.

In space, however, astronauts do not have this atmosphere to keep them safe, so they are constantly bombarded with solar and cosmic radiation. Without protection, astronauts would almost certainly develop radiation sickness or cancer. To protect astronauts from these dangers, spacecraft, space stations, and even spacesuits are constructed with shielding that reduces astronauts' exposure to radiation.

Under some conditions, however, the astronauts' shielding would not be enough. For example, when a solar flare occurs, the level of radiation in space is much higher than normal. If astronauts were caught by a solar flare while out on a spacewalk, they would be in big trouble; their suits would not protect them. Astronauts on board the station itself would have to retreat to special *storm shelters*, heavily shielded compartments that block extra radiation.

International Space Station

Still under construction, the *International Space Station* will be the largest human-made object in space when it is complete. The station grew out of an earlier project, a proposed space station called *Freedom*. The United States began plans to build *Freedom* in the 1980s but then scaled the plans back for budgetary reasons. Along the way, the United States took on partners, including Canada; a number of European countries; Japan; and, eventually, Russia. This spirit of international cooperation allows these countries to share both the work of building the station and the benefits to come from research conducted there.

Eventually there will be six laboratories, most of which will likely be dedicated to biological research and the processing of medicines and electrical components. The finished station will have more than four times as much room as any previous space station. In fact, it will be so big that, when it is completed in 2004, it will be visible from Earth.

13

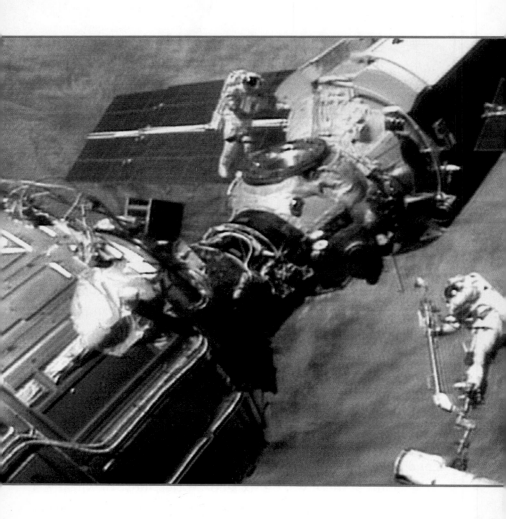

Future Space Stations

Scientists may yet figure out a way to make space more livable. Future habitats could become large enough for many people to live in without feeling cramped. Perhaps shields will be developed that effectively block dangerous radiation so that citizens of space colonies will be as safe as people on Earth. In addition, if these stations are spun to create gravity, bone loss may no longer be as serious a danger as it is for astronauts today.

Now that there is an established workplace in space, it will be easier for countries to build new space stations, using the *International Space Station* as a launching pad. Parts could be flown up from Earth and assembled by the station crews.

Countries will be able to construct larger and more elaborate stations or even outfit new spacecraft that can journey to the moon or perhaps Mars. A trip to the moon wouldn't be as hard to accomplish from a launch pad in space because the spacecraft wouldn't have to fight Earth's gravity to lift off. Instead of filling valuable cargo space with rocket fuel, scientists could fill these crafts with research instruments. The possibilities are endless.

Whatever solutions humans come up with to make life in orbit more sustainable over the long term, one thing is certain: Space is only going to get more and more populated in the coming decades. Zero-gravity manufacturing promises many benefits over Earth-bound manufacturing, and private companies may soon be subsidizing experiments in space or even sending their own people into orbit to do high-tech work that is impossible on Earth.

Does this sound far-fetched? Well, some of these things may happen within a year or two. Perhaps one day soon people will routinely be able to buy passenger seats on a spacecraft for a vacation in space. Maybe students will be able to attend college on a space station. Imagine telvision game shows with visits to a space station as one of the prizes!

How would you feel about joining a group of your friends for a trip into space one day? Do you think you would enjoy life on a space station?